Love
Aline ♡
Every Moment Matters!

Huge Love!

LISTEN UP!
YOUR *Heart* IS SPEAKING

ROBIN LEE

BALBOA.
PRESS

A DIVISION OF HAY HOUSE

Balboa Press books may be ordered through booksellers or by contacting:

Balboa Press
A Division of Hay House
1663 Liberty Drive
Bloomington, IN 47403
www.balboapress.com
1 (877) 407-4847

Because of the dynamic nature of the Internet, any web addresses or
links contained in this book may have changed since publication and
may no longer be valid. The views expressed in this work are solely those
of the author and do not necessarily reflect the views of the publisher,
and the publisher hereby disclaims any responsibility for them.

The author of this book does not dispense medical advice or prescribe
the use of any technique as a form of treatment for physical, emotional,
or medical problems without the advice of a physician, either directly
or indirectly. The intent of the author is only to offer information
of a general nature to help you in your quest for emotional and
spiritual well-being. In the event you use any of the information in
this book for yourself, which is your constitutional right, the author
and the publisher assume no responsibility for your actions.

Any people depicted in stock imagery provided by Thinkstock are
models, and such images are being used for illustrative purposes only.
Certain stock imagery © Thinkstock.

Print information available on the last page.

ISBN: 978-1-5043-6936-7 (sc)
ISBN: 978-1-5043-6934-3 (hc)
ISBN: 978-1-5043-6935-0 (e)

Library of Congress Control Number: 2016958676

Balboa Press rev. date: 12/08/2016

Contents

Acknowledgments

This creation was made possible because of the incredible love and support I received from my family and friends. There are a few people I would like to acknowledge because without them, this book would still be sitting in my desk drawer.

My beautiful daughters, Kanya and Vismaya, for their strength and faith. They are the wind beneath my wings!

My mother, Gail Hoehn, for being kind and understanding with me every day. She's not only my mom, but manages my entire practice. I wouldn't be where I am today without her help, love, and support.

Larry and Valery Hoehn, for helping me stay focused on what matters most and reminding me not to get distracted by things that leave me uninspired.

Spencer Parkes, for daily reminders that following my Heart will never steer me wrong and will only lead to better and better experiences.

Maritza Puello, for keeping my chin up, for dowsing me with essential oils when I was spaced out and scattered, and for being my spokesperson over and over again in the process of birthing this book. Her gentleness and patience keeping me focused are quite admirable. Thank you!

Deirdre McKenna, for always believing in me and my intuitive abilities.

Brandy Fleming, for reminding me that when we are simply kind, life will always reward us. We are never, ever given any more than we can handle.

My Healthy Habits community members for creating a space for us to share our day-to-day experiences without judgment.

I also wanted to thank everyone who supported my IndieGogo campaign. I want to give some extra grateful vibes to the following IndieGogo contributors:

Derek Bone

Tanna Kelton

Marianne P. Milevoi

The Abbasi Family

The McKenna Family

Larry and Valery Hoehn

Sarah Gordon

Julie Murray

Angie Van Cleaf

Eve Hornstein

Merryl Weber

Susan and Bob Wohl

Sandy Cascone

Jeane Wallace

Rowan Beck

Leslie Meenan

Constance Lehmann

Orli Spanier

Melinda London

Cynthia DeMonte

Denise Johnson

Rosemary Alexander

Ellen Furman

Thank you all from the bottom of my Heart!

Introduction

I remember the moment I decided to write this book. I was sitting on a bench at the mall, people-watching, and was taken aback by the look on most people's faces as they walked by. What looked like preoccupation, worry, exhaustion, and stress seemed to dominate them.

I became overwhelmed with emotion when I noticed this, and I knew I had something to share that could make a difference in these and many other people's lives. In my years of practice as a Medical Intuitive, I spend hours a day guiding people to pay attention to the quality of life that they have created and helping them understand how it relates to their physical health and emotional well- being. I knew that the unhappiness I witnessed that day in the mall on people's faces could be transformed by empowering each of them to remember to honor how they feel before making the daily decisions that impact the overall quality of their lives. I sat down with a paper and pen, and began writing.

Inside each of us is a unique voice that, if listened

to, will create everything we could ever dream of. It is never too late to listen to our inner wisdom or to change our life's course.

You are worthy and capable of living a happy and inspired life. The information I will share in this book will give you the tools to start living your Heart's desire and creating a life you truly love.

Chapter 1

Connecting with Your Heart

Your Heart speaks to you all the time. Every day, every night, every minute. Are you listening to it? Do you know how to do that? Shh. Take a moment. Close your eyes. Take a deep breath, inhaling in through the nose, exhaling out through the mouth. Listen. What is your Heart saying to you?

Inside your Heart sits a vast amount of information. This knowledge can help you live a truly inspired life. Some call this intuition, some call it inspiration, and some call it simple awareness. Whatever you may call it, please remember, it is your Heart speaking to you.

You may think you can't connect to your Heart, or perhaps you believe that only if you have a special gift can you establish that connection. You have that special gift. As long as your Heart beats, I promise you, you have it. This special gift is called being alive. Your heartbeat connects you to the wisdom of the generations that lived before you as well as the heartbeat of our planet. Once you experience this for yourself, you will know this to be true too.

I believe that spirituality is life itself because as you commit to connecting to your Heart, every moment you are alive is an opportunity to grow closer to yourself and to be able to receive the answers to any questions that come before you.

Writing this book is a dream come true for me. Ever since I was a little girl, I wanted to be an author. Now is the perfect time for me to sit and share with you some things I have learned over the years. The ideas and techniques I will share have worked for me and for the thousands of people I have worked with over the years.

Know that you are feeling connected to explore this book for a reason. Enjoy it! Nobody knows what is best for you except you. You find your truth by honoring what resonates inside of you and by being able to muster up the courage to honor these simple things.

You may be thinking, *Easier said than done.* Many of you don't feel like you can hear your Heart or have any idea how to distinguish the difference between your thoughts and your Heart's wisdom. Slow down for a minute. Stop. Shh. Take a big, deep breath, and allow yourself to be still.

Close your eyes, listen for your heartbeat, and

breathe. Can you feel the rhythm of your Heart? Breathe in deeply. Breathe in through your nose and out through your mouth. Focus on your heartbeat. Can you begin to feel the stillness? Try it again. This stillness is the gateway to your Heart.

Affirmation:

My Heart speaks to me.

Chapter 2

Anchoring into Your Heart

How can connecting with your Heart help you create anything you want? By connecting to your Heart, you honor its innate wisdom. You know knowledge is power, and with that comes the force to create.

To resonate with your Heart, you must take time to connect to it consciously and to become familiar with the way it feels. Build a relationship with it. But where do you start? To have a healthy relationship with your Heart, you need to prioritize spending time with yourself. This is the most important thing I could share with you. I will repeat that: prioritize spending time with your Heart!

You can't expect your Heart to find its own place in your life. Remember, it is your responsibility to slow down and create a space in your life for your Heart. Creating space for what is important to you is a simple way to honor the connection to what you say you love and respect. Own the process!

Regret usually comes from the moment when you forget to honor yourself and instead take things, events, and people for granted. Perhaps you have not been taught to pay attention. You have been taught to honor the opinions of others and society instead of the wisdom of your own experience and being.

Your entire life is based on your consistent habits. Perhaps listening to your Heart is as simple as making a daily habit of spending time with yourself. How wonderful would it be if it were that easy? Actually, it is.

You may be used to waking up to a blaring alarm clock, thinking about the monstrous number of daily tasks you will need to do, checking your e-mails or text messages—and all of this within five minutes of waking up. It's likely you jump in the shower, grab a cup of coffee, and jet out the door to begin the day with a feeling of dread and of being overwhelmed. Starting your days like this will *not* be conducive to learning how to resonate with your Heart or hear it speak. In fact, it will be impossible to hear your Heart when you start your days like this.

Your Heart speaks in stillness, and when it speaks, it's usually very clear. All you have to do is be still and listen.

How can you make a conscious effort to create more stillness in your morning routine? First, choose to make your Heart connection a priority. You can't just say, "I don't have the time." Make the time. To have stillness, your home doesn't need to feel like a church on a Sunday morning. The idea is simply to make a little time for yourself and not feel pressured from the moment your eyes open first thing in the morning.

Consider purchasing an alarm clock that gently wakes you up without a frightening jolt. A jolt scares the Heart and creates a feeling of panic and pressure that you begin your day with. Have you thought about this simple idea? It may not seem like a big deal, because you are used to waking up abruptly. It is a habit you have gotten used to. Actually, it is a huge deal when you want to learn how to resonate with your Heart. Feelings of pressure and stress affect the central nervous system and create tension in the body. This tension creates fear and inflammation.

When you wake up suddenly in the morning, your day begins with a fear-filled, stressful experience. So your wake-up routine is the perfect place to start building a harmonious connection to your Heart. Wake up with gentleness and ease.

Before checking your e-mails or text messages, and even before getting out of bed, consider what you want to experience that day. How do you want to feel? Take a few minutes to anchor yourself into your Heart. Simply find your pulse on your neck, wrist, or chest. Close your eyes and focus on taking slow, deep breaths. As you breathe in through your nose and out through your mouth, notice the beat of your Heart.

Take as many breaths as you have to before your focus shifts to your heartbeat. Be patient with yourself. Your focus has been outside of yourself for quite some time. You may find it takes time to connect to your Heart. Once you find its steady beat, pay attention to the stillness this connection creates.

Slow down your breathing even more. There is no rush. Give yourself permission to relax. Slowly and deeply inhale through your nose and exhale slowly out through your mouth. Imagine that with each inhalation through your nose, peace and stillness enter into every cell of your body. As you slowly exhale through your mouth, feel pressure and stress leave your body.

With each breath, you are anchoring into the feeling of your Heart. As you experience this stillness, you are beginning to resonate with your Heart. Our bodies, minds, and spirits crave stillness.

The quality of your life comes from the choices that you make. If you want stillness and peace, do things that create stillness and peace. You must not wait for them to come looking for you. Anchoring into your Heart creates stillness and a deep feeling of peace, confidence, and relaxation. You will notice a feeling of safety begin to grow because you are empowering yourself. You are committing to creating the quality of life that you want instead of mindlessly anchoring into the concerns and chaos of your daily life, which can leave you feeling ripped off, empty, and unhappy. How can you expect to be fulfilled if you are disconnected from your Heart and take no action to positively fuel the relationship with it that you want to experience?

As you breathe, please remember to pay attention

to feeling your heartbeat, and allow yourself to experience it. The stable beat of your Heart continues every moment of every day without you having to be concerned about it or focus on it. Isn't this incredible?

Pay attention to the calm stillness that begins to take over as you connect to your heartbeat. There is a knowing trust that comes from connecting to your Heart. With each breath you take, give yourself permission to breathe in the feeling of strength and serenity. Allow yourself to relax and trust. Let go of pressure. You will easily hear your Heart if you allow yourself to open up and relax. Be patient, consistent, gentle, kind, and understanding of yourself.

Affirmation:

I am connected to my Heart.

Chapter 3

Resonating with Your Heart

As you learn to resonate with your Heart, you will want to focus consciously on the way your Heart feels. When you are learning to relate with something new, typically you will slow down, pay attention, and put effort toward connecting to whatever you want to resonate with. Relationships don't just happen. They take time, commitment, and focus.

If you forget to spend time with your Heart, you may begin to feel lost. Your being is just like a ship in the ocean during a harsh storm. When you reconnect into your Heart, you will begin to feel calm even in the middle of chaos. When you feel calm in the middle of chaos, you know you have found the key to creating the quality of your life.

Every thought of the day can throw you around the sea of confusion and disharmony if you forget to anchor yourself into the safe stillness of your Heart.

Some people have told me it can't be that easy. It is, if you remember to slow down, breathe, find your heartbeat, and allow yourself to feel its stillness. Be consistent with making your relationship with your Heart a priority, and you will be pleasantly surprised by how easy is it to hear your Heart speak.

The quality of your life comes from the choices you make. When you allow yourself to make choices that support how you want to feel, you begin to feel empowered. If you want to feel loved, happy, and joyous, allow yourself to feel the emotion of love as you go about your daily routine and do things with a loving attitude. It sounds simple, doesn't it? That's because it is. The quality of your life is created by the choices you make.

We are Heart-centered beings. Pretend that your Heart is the home that you live in. Imagine having no home to go to at night to rest and rejuvenate. How would you feel? Tired? Lonely? Anxious? Angry? Scared? Fearful? Disconnected? Depressed? Some people struggle with these feelings on a daily basis.

When those feelings arise, it's a reminder to connect right back to your Heart and allow those uncomfortable feelings to begin to melt away. Remember to nurture this process so that you can feel with your Heart and hear when it speaks.

You might say you don't have enough time in your day to check in with your Heart. I get it. I really get it. I am a single mom of two beautiful girls, with a busy career and a passion to enjoy my life. I also really enjoy my sleep.

Please hear this with the gentle intention that it is being shared with: You can keep making excuses as to why you can't do what's necessary to commit to creating what you want. Coming up with excuses is easy to do. I know because I did it for years. Please do yourself a favor and stop saying you want something different in your life if you are not willing to do anything differently. Each time you say you want something and don't put effort in that direction, you will feel like a victim and a failure. You don't deserve to feel that way. When you are ready to commit to change, you will. Just remember to be gentle with yourself.

Consider that you are brilliantly guided and supported in your life, and for some reason you were led to read this right now. Everything happens in the perfect time. Just relax. Give yourself a break, and stop putting pressure on yourself.

You can easily get hooked on the hamster wheel of unconsciously living your life. You just start your day without thinking about how you want to feel and what you really want to experience. If everything feels secure, safe, and easy, but you feel bored or out of sorts, it's an indicator you aren't connected to your Heart.

If you want a different experience or outcome, simply make different choices and take different actions. If you don't do this, you will have the same experience over and over again. By remembering this, you declare to the world, to the universe, and most importantly to yourself, "This is my life, my creation. I am ready, willing and able to take full responsibility for the quality of my life."

If you are like most people, so often you forget that you can consciously choose what you do and focus on. Allow your life to become simple. Make choices that feel good to you. Become conscious of your Heart by slowing down, stepping back, and finding the place of calm before making decisions. Your Heart is waiting to guide you to a profoundly joyful life.

Affirmation:

I choose to make the relationship
with my Heart a priority.

Chapter 4

Making the Moment Matter

Now that you understand the idea of connecting to your Heart, remember that slowing down is the key to building that connection.

Slowing down means choosing to create moments that really matter to you. The next time you notice pressure, tension, anxiety, irritation, or stress, that moment is offering you a tremendous gift.

Stop. Look. Listen. Choose.

Simply notice what you are feeling. In that moment you can shift your focus and have a different experience. When you feel uncomfortable, take a slow deep breath, and gently give yourself permission to relax and slow down.

The more you are present, the more you will breathe deeply and the more naturally you will begin to experience joy and happiness.

Slowing down is choosing to make ordinary moments in your life extraordinary, to become conscious of what you are doing, and to know you are responsible for creating the quality of these moments. When feelings of discomfort arise, it can be a reminder that you have gotten distracted and your Heart is reminding you to refocus.

Have you ever been asked what you had for breakfast and you simply couldn't remember? That is probably because you were doing ten things at once and most likely thinking about twenty-two other things at the same time. Rushing around is a habit that keeps you from being able to connect to your Heart throughout the day.

What does slowing down have to do with being able to hear the language of your Heart? The feeling of being uncomfortable is caused by unexpressed emotions. Next time you feel unsettled, slow down, take a deep breath, and ask your Heart what it's feeling. When you ask a question and are willing to listen, you will be able to hear your Heart speak. *Always!*

The next time you feel uneasy, take a deep breath and ask how you can make the moment in front of you matter.

Imagine walking into a room where there are ten television sets on. How do you think you would feel after twenty minutes? Do you think you would feel calm and relaxed, or do you think you may feel anxious and unable to focus on any one station?

You are more than capable of easily hearing your Heart speak; there are just too many channels on at one time.

Perhaps you have forgotten that you can hear your Heart whenever you choose to listen to it. If you want to connect, you simply need to remember to take a deep breath, spend some time with yourself, and ask for wisdom and insight. When you take time for yourself, you are quickly reminded that *you* matter. Taking time for yourself creates confidence and trust between you and your Heart.

People often voice concern that if they focus on slowing down, they will become less productive. The opposite is true. When you learn to anchor in your own Heart, time has a way of slowing down, and more can be accomplished in a shorter amount of time.

Why is it so hard to slow down? As in other areas in life, we have gotten stuck in habits that simply aren't conducive to creating a wonderful quality of life.

Consider feeling ever so blessed the next time you say or think, "I am stressed" or "I am pressured."

Right in this moment, you have an opportunity to create a new experience. Every time you become aware that you feel pressured or stressed, you are being given a chance to empower yourself.

Stop. Look. Listen. Choose.

Create a positive change for yourself.

You can create more joy for yourself in ordinary moments by remembering to slow down. What can you think of incorporating into your day to make ordinary moments extraordinary?

The good experiences you live don't create themselves. You do. Life has a funny way of creating situations that feel stressful, pressured, and overwhelming to remind you to pause, take a gigantic breath, and focus on something that you can enjoy in the moment before you.

Consider trying it the next time you are stuck in traffic and feeling all twisted and tangled. Take a deep breath, and remind yourself that life may be offering you an intimate moment to spend with yourself.

Ask yourself, "What can I notice about my surroundings right now that I typically wouldn't notice?" Empower yourself by seeking to find the blessings in the moment.

Stress is an opportunity to slow down and breathe. Remember, breathing is the bridge that connects you to your Heart and the beauty that sits before you in your life. In every moment that you create joy, you build a bond between yourself and your Heart.

The feelings and experiences that you have been hoping and waiting to receive are right in front of and within you. Remember to slow down, breathe, and create joy in the moment.

With each moment that passes, may you have the confidence to say, "I am endlessly supported in my life."

Affirmation:

Every moment supports me.

Chapter 5

Gratitude

As you learn to slow down, you begin to realize your life is full of incredible beauty.

Each time you acknowledge the beauty around you, your Heart is able to relax and open up a little bit more. Life is precious. Remember that, and remind those around you to focus on all the beautiful things to be grateful for that make life sweeter than it would be without them.

Learn to train your mind to be forever grateful. Gratitude is a powerful habit that quickly opens up communication with your Heart. The habit of gratitude is absolutely essential in helping consistently nurture your relationship with your Heart.

Many times over, people all over the world have told me that they have nothing to be grateful for. Most of those people share stories of great loss: divorce, bankruptcy, death, illness, just to name a few. I always invite people who share these stories with me to consider all of life as temporary. When you are reminded of this, not only do you live a more full and expansive life, you also feel more present, still, and supported by what is happening in your life. Gratitude helps you to be present and to let go of yesterday's regrets and worries about tomorrow.

People often call me "Pollyanna" and ask if I have ever been through really hard times. I am consistently taken aback by that. Of course I have been through hard times. The difference is I choose to see the gift or lesson that is available in challenging times.

I am committed to staying connected to my Heart, regardless of what is happening, which allows me to feel peaceful. It is an absolute priority for me. I constantly remind myself that life is in constant flux and that how I choose to live those moments is what creates the quality of my life. I have been through many incredibly difficult and challenging times. I know what it feels like to not want to get out of bed, and I know what it feels like to not have anything to be grateful for.

One thing I can tell you for certain is that the most difficult times in my life have given me the biggest gifts and lessons because I took them as an opportunity to learn something new. Until you are willing to see the blessing in moments that are painful, you can't begin to heal.

There is always something to be grateful for. When I remind myself that things could be worse, it is often easier to find the gratitude in things.

I'm not saying that what you are going through isn't incredibly painful. It's essential to allow yourself to feel whatever emotion is present, but please remember not to get stuck in the feeling for too long. Don't pretend the situation isn't going to change. Everything changes. It is one of my favorite promises that life has to offer. When things seem near impossible to get through, I find incredible peace in telling myself that nothing lasts forever.

You truly are never given anything more than you can handle. You know those days when you can barely get out of bed? You know those moments when you feel like you are going to completely lose your cool? Take a big, deep breath. Create an intention for the next inhalation to give you strength and your exhalation to remove some of the tension you are feeling. Ask the breath to give you clarity and confidence. Focus on your surroundings. Slow down. Breathe again. Tell yourself, "I am stronger and more capable than I realize."

Take another deep breath, and focus on three things to be grateful for. Notice the incredible resistance to focusing on things to be grateful for when you feel unmotivated. Connect to your feelings deeply, but shift your focus to three things you are grateful for.

When you focus on those specific things you are grateful for, something interesting happens. Each thought of gratitude is a seed that grows inside of your Heart over time. People often say to me, "Yeah, so what? What are seeds of gratitude? What's the big deal?" When your mind is full of gratitude, it is easier to feel positive things are going to happen during the day. This is one of the gifts of focusing on gratitude. Harder times naturally become easier.

I remember years ago trying to fall asleep as I thought about my worries and concerns. Through the practice of gratitude, I was able to realize that worry is a choice. It's natural to feel worry about what you can't control. How nice would it be to assume the best will happen? When you focus on gratitude, naturally you will learn to expect the best over time. Worry will begin to dissolve.

Gratitude is a key that opens up the doorway to your Heart. When you are anchored in your Heart, you live in a space of acceptance, trust, and confidence.

Exactly how does gratitude support you to be able to hear your Heart speaking? When you experience gratitude, you experience acceptance. Acceptance is surrendering to the moment and trusting that what is happening is in your best interest. Acceptance creates stillness in your Heart and mind.

Every night before you go to bed, focus on three things that you are grateful for. I have been expressing gratitude daily for many years. At first, when I began this practice, it was very hard for me to find things to be grateful for.

I had a journal that sat underneath my bed. Before I turned my light off at night, I would take my journal out and focus on three things I was grateful for. At first I didn't notice much of a difference. As I continued with my gratitude commitment, I noticed the changes in how I related to people and situations in life.

The experiences I had were similar to the ones

that I read about in spiritual teachings. I felt happy, content, safe, confident, at peace, and supported. I noticed I had more compassion and less judgment. The most incredible thing I remember was that these feelings and experiences just happened. Gratitude heals because it connects you to the wisdom of your Heart.

I didn't change my diet, go on a fast, or meditate for hours to experience these changes. I made a commitment to focus on three things to be grateful for every night, whether or not I wanted to. That is all I did.

From the bottom of my Heart, I urge you to focus on making gratitude part of your daily habit, even if it is hard to do at first. I promise that you will see a tremendous difference over time. You will grow more connected to your Heart.

Affirmation:

I am grateful for every moment of my life.

Chapter 6

The Heart and the Mind

Here is a question I imagine you are thinking as you read this book: How can I tell the difference between my Heart and my mind speaking?

Hearing the Heart speak is much easier than you may think. There are qualities of the Heart and qualities of the mind. The difficult part about differentiating between your Heart and your mind is remembering to slow down enough to connect and feel the difference.

The Heart's language tells you what choices to make to be able to feel fully alive and vibrant. The mind's language guides you to make choices to be able to survive in the world—and not much more. As you gain experience living in your Heart's wisdom, your life will become easier and more flowing, joyful, and full of synchronicity.

As you connect to your Heart, in time you will become more confident and optimistic. But easier doesn't mean that everything will go according to your wishes or as you have planned. You may be used to making decisions based on what your mind is telling you is right or wrong, which is based on what you have been taught from your parents, your environment, your society, and even your own fears. You let pros and cons ping-pong back and forth, and eventually you make a decision that makes the most logical sense. You often try to make decisions based on what you think will create the least amount of pain and keep you in the safety zone.

Remember to anchor your thoughts in your Heart by breathing deeply and slowing down. See how your Heart feels about these thoughts. How things feel to your Heart matters *a lot*. When you start to dissect how things feel, you begin to experience freedom and joy, which are quite liberating. When you give yourself permission to feel, you remind yourself that your opinion matters, and you immediately begin to feel optimistic and hopeful because you are reminding yourself that you always have a choice.

When you forget to connect into your Heart, you are unconsciously making decisions based on fear. You may fear making the wrong decision because of what others may say or think about you, and you may be afraid of being judged.

There will be times when you will get an expansive feeling in your Heart when something doesn't make any logical sense whatsoever. You will notice a relaxed feeling in your Heart but a war inside your mind. Ask yourself, "What am I afraid of?" Remember to breathe, and take some time to anchor back into yourself. Your Heart always knows what is best for you and your personal evolution.

When you trust your intuition and make difficult choices, it is important to define the reason *why* you are making the decision at hand. Just because you listen to your Heart doesn't mean you will have a painless experience of bliss and perfection. The beauty of listening to your Heart is that you have given yourself a choice. Your intention to choose to listen to your Heart and what happens after that is perfect for your evolution.

Important decisions are normally extremely difficult to make, especially when you want a certain outcome. It's important not to be attached to what the outcome will be. For example, if you choose to pursue a relationship and the relationship ends, it doesn't mean it wasn't worth going after or that you made a wrong decision.

Life happens. It isn't about doing the right thing

and having a "good" outcome. It's simply about being able to remember that you are responsible for the quality of life that you live. Taking responsibility for your choices is the first part of that.

When things don't go the way you want them to, that means you have lessons to learn and something even better is on its way. When things don't go the way you want, don't doubt your choice. Outcomes have nothing to do with you making the right or wrong decision. Take a breath, and ask your Heart what new lesson this situation is offering to you.

Strive to have confidence when making decisions. Self-doubt removes a lot of joy from your days. It is a filter you often look through that constantly waits for something to "prove you wrong." There is no right. There is no wrong. There is only choosing to follow your Heart or choosing to follow your mind.

Regardless, remember that it is a choice. If things don't work out the way you want them to, it simply means there is some learning that is available to you. That's all. It has nothing to do with making a mistake. In order to hear the wisdom of your Heart, let go of judgment.

Stop holding your breath, hoping you are going to do things right and fearing something bad is going to happen if you make a wrong decision. Muster up the courage to trust yourself and be readily available to take full responsibility for the quality of your life. Be willing to think for yourself instead of consistently comparing yourself to what others around you are doing. Let go of needing acknowledgment from the outside. Close your eyes, center yourself, and seek acknowledgment from within.

You have your own unique path that only you know. Listening to your Heart has to do with making the most out of your life and honoring the moment for the incredible gift that it is.

In order to walk the path of the Heart, be willing to let go of the fear of not fitting in and getting into trouble. Replace it with confidence that life has your back and will always support you more than you could ever imagine.

Listening to your Heart speak is a wonderful habit to cultivate and a guaranteed way to create a happier and more fulfilled life.

How do you know when your Heart is speaking?

It is when you feel loving, joyful, grateful, strong, gentle, understanding, patient, relaxed, optimistic, excitement, peaceful, energetic, expansive, connected, harmonious, calm, clear, confident, trusting, compassionate.

How do you know when your mind is speaking? It is when you feel fearful, doubtful, pessimistic, overwhelmed, jealous, nervous, anxious, rushed, concerned, worried, lacking, irritable, tense, confused, restricted, frustrated, stressed, judgmental, exhausted, unsettled.

As you sit with yourself and notice that your mind is speaking, take several slow, deep breaths, and ask yourself what you are afraid of. Listen for the answers. When you allow your fear to be acknowledged, you gently slide right back into your Heart. Trusting your Heart takes time. The walls of fear can run very high inside of you.

Be gentle and patient with yourself.

Affirmation:

I confidently make wonderful
decisions for myself.

Chapter 7

Breathing through the Fear

When it comes down to it, it's difficult to listen to your Heart because you are afraid to do so.

It is also a bit tricky because you probably haven't had anyone guide you on the journey toward your Heart. As unique as you are, your path is just as unique. When you feel confused and feel the beat of your Heart, you will be able to relax and listen to the wisdom your Heart is offering.

Fear and feeling tied down are the nature of the mind. Love and feeling free and expansive are the nature of the Heart. Where there is love, fear will dissolve. Any time you do something new, you are going to feel both fear and excitement. It is incredibly important that you feel fear deeply and listen to the words that fear uses to threaten you. If you try to ignore or silence fear, it will become louder and create tension and anxiety. When we give fear a voice and learn to empathize and understand it, over time the intensity of the fear softens.

When you acknowledge the fear and really feel it, you then can choose what to do with it. The more you pretend that you are not afraid or try to ignore the fear, the greater the grasp that fear will have on you. Isn't this the truth with many things? That which you try to minimize eventually begins to rule you. How much easier is it for you to simply be honest with how you feel?

When you focus on connecting with your Heart, that connection strengthens and grows. It really is that simple.

Listening to your Heart is simply giving yourself permission to slow down and simplify your life, spending time doing things you love with people you love. If you create a life of love, of course it will be easy to feel connected to your Heart.

What happens in your life isn't based on good or bad behavior or on you having made a right or wrong decision. How easy or difficult life is depends on how you choose to define things. If you choose to say that when things don't go the way you want, you have failed or made a wrong decision; life is going to be filled with fear and stress. In fact, you will never really stop holding your breath, hoping that you have done well and are good enough.

Consider not allowing fear to overtake your peace of mind. Remind yourself that peace comes from perspective, and perspective is your decision and your choice.

Our Hearts hold no fear. When fear comes close to your Heart, its energy melts any fear away. Breathe your fear into your Heart, and let your Heart do the rest. If you want to live in harmony, you must feel fear and have the courage to let it go.

I am so very excited for you to live a Heart-inspired life!

Affirmation:

I choose to let go of fear.

Chapter 8

Heart Connection Exercises

Following are some exercises you can do to build and strengthen the Heart connection you are seeking.

Just like consistently going to the gym will make your muscles more defined, doing these exercises will strengthen the connection to your Heart.

There isn't a right or wrong way to do these exercises. They have an accumulating effect, so do them as often as you feel inspired to. Remember, if an event or situation feels like it's creating pressure or stress, it's a great opportunity to take a breath and try one of these exercises. Ask questions. Breathe. Listen. Your Heart is speaking to you!

Exercise 1: Hands On

Lie down on your back and get comfortable. Close your eyes. Gently place your left hand on your stomach and your right hand on your chest.

Slowly and deeply breathe in through your nose and out through your mouth. After taking a few deep breaths, use your next inhalation to allow yourself to visualize a bright-orange color moving deeply into your body. When you feel like you can't inhale anymore, hold your breath for a count of four and slowly, with control, exhale through your mouth, visualizing a murky-orange color leaving your body.

Repeat this simple exercise for about five minutes. The slower and more controlled you breathe, the more connected you will become to your Heart.

FAQs

Why do I breathe in through the nose and out through the mouth in this exercise?

Breathing this way helps your physical body to relax and release tension, stress, and negative energy. With this exercise, you will notice your stomach feeling lighter and less restricted.

Why do I put my hands on my stomach and my Heart?

Our stomachs hold a lot of tension in our day-to-day lives. Have you noticed when you are under stress or around highly stressed people that your digestion becomes sensitive or uncomfortable? When you place your hands on your stomach, you are giving strength and energy to that specific area.

You may be used to holding onto a great deal of

stress and tension, especially in your belly, which takes energy away from other parts of your body. By placing one hand on your belly and the other on your Heart, you are creating a healthy circuit that allows for a greater level of energy to flow. When you put your hands on your body, it keeps energy from going out and helps keep the energy circulating inside of yourself. This is a very powerful tool that immediately soothes and relaxes your body as well as your mind.

How often can I do this?

As often as you like! This exercise is especially helpful if you are feeling worried or concerned, or if something is weighing on your mind. Just lie down, and do the breathing exercise.

Exercise 2: Journaling

Journaling is one of my favorite exercises when I feel anxious and overwhelmed. There is a profound connection and truth available to us when we "get things off our chest."

Before you begin to journal, start by practicing exercise 1, above, for about five minutes. Once you notice your mind beginning to calm down and feel more relaxed, you can begin writing.

Allow yourself to write whatever comes to mind. Don't hold yourself back. Just give yourself permission to write. When you allow your mind to be acknowledged, it will naturally begin to quiet down and make it easier for you to feel your Heart and hear it speak.

When you finish writing, take a deep breath, close your eyes, and honor how you feel inside.

Now that you have gotten all those thoughts on paper that have been weighing you down, you will feel lighter, and it will be easier to hear your Heart speak. It is absolutely essential that you take a minute or two after your writing to explore how you feel inside. What do you notice? Take a deep breath and honor everything that you feel.

FAQs

Do I have to write on paper, or is it okay to use my computer or device?

It's essential to use a pen and paper.

Does it matter what hand I write with?

It does matter a lot. Write with your nondominant hand. I know it will seem very awkward at first, but it is important that you journal with this hand.

Why is it important that I write with my nondominant hand?

Just because writing with both hands doesn't come easily doesn't mean we shouldn't use both hands in our lives. Our dominant hand speaks more from a logical place, and our nondominant hand naturally shares from a more emotional place. When we honor how we feel, it is much easier to allow our Heart to guide us and to keep a clear, Heart-centered perspective.

Exercise 3: Tarzaning

Gently tap your chest, as though you were Tarzan. Be *gentle*. This means *no pounding*! As you gently tap your chest, breathe slowly and deeply in through your nose. As you exhale through your mouth, say the syllable *ahhhhhhh*. This literally opens up the energy of your Heart, both physically and energetically.

One or two minutes should be enough to be able

to activate this part of your body. Feel free to do it as often as you want. Just close your eyes and start tapping with both hands, back and forth, saying *ahhhh* every time you exhale. This is a very simple yet powerful exercise to help activate and open your Heart's center.

FAQs

I've been tapping for a few days now and don't feel anything.

Don't be discouraged. Have patience. Be consistent. Sometimes it takes time to feel the connection with your Heart.

Sometimes I want to tap when I am around other people, like at work or lunch. Can I tap and not make a sound?

Yes, you can, but tapping with sound is more productive.

I felt a big wave of emotion come up as I was tapping. Is that okay?

Yes, that is normal. Keep breathing slowly. If you feel you need to release an emotion, do so.

Does this really work to help open up the energy of my Heart?

Most definitely so. Before you begin tapping, just close your eyes and get a sense of how you feel in your chest. As you begin to tap, observe how you feel. You will most likely notice your chest vibrating or feeling more alive.

When people working with physical heart and breast issues come to me, this is one of the first things we do to support the body's energy system to be able to heal from the inside out. Stagnation is the true issue for all dis-ease and imbalance. Let's get things moving.

Exercise 4: Massage the Chest

Carefully place one drop of pure sandalwood essential oil or pure rose oil in the center of your palms, and rub your palms until they feel warm. When you notice this warmth, close your eyes and gently lift your palms to your nose. Slowly inhale the scent of essential oil. Do this for a few deep breaths. Once you have completed this, gently massage your chest in a circular motion from right to left.

Big circles, small circles—it really doesn't matter. Just put your hand on your chest and gently start moving your hand in a circular motion from right to left.

Breathe as slowly and as deeply as you can, in through your nose and out through your mouth. With a gentle touch, massage whatever area of your chest you feel drawn to. Make sure to focus on what you are doing. Be aware. Be gentle. These are moments spent being kind and present with yourself. Times spent like this are very nourishing to your body, mind, and spirit.

Life can be hard and abrasive. Your body builds up defenses in and around your Heart area. This exercise is important because it allows you to relax your body. When you relax into your body, you will be able to experience your feelings more deeply.

This exercise is an easy and gentle way to tune in and remind yourself that you are safe, nurtured, and loved every moment of every day.

FAQs

Is there an ideal amount of time to do this exercise?

Three to five minutes is ideal.

Is it best for me to massage directly on my skin or on top of my clothes?

It doesn't matter. What feels most nurturing? Do that.

Can I use more than one drop of an essential oil?

I wouldn't recommend it. Essential oils are very concentrated, and using too much might make the skin a bit irritated. Remember, gentleness is a key to healing.

Exercise 5: Grounding

Stand on the grass, dirt, or sand with bare feet. As you casually stand there, place your left hand on your chest and your right hand on top of it.

Close your eyes, breathe slowly in through your nose, and exhale out through your mouth. Just breathe. Relax your shoulders. Keep your hands on your chest.

As you stand with your bare feet on the ground, the earth will naturally share its healing energy with you by coming up through the bottoms of your feet and entering into your body as you inhale.

The positive energy coming into your body will begin to dissolve anything that no longer serves you. As you slowly exhale, the earth will absorb anything that your body no longer needs to hold onto.

The earth is an incredible filtration system if you take the time to connect to her. Notice as you do this the feelings that you experience. Joy, peace, and a sense of belonging are common.

FAQs

I live in a cold climate, what do I do?

Don't do this exercise until the weather is warm enough.

Is there a better time than another to do this exercise?

Mornings and early evenings are the ideal times to do this exercise. Steer away from it during the late morning and afternoon.

The energy that nature shares with us greatly affects us. When the sun is the least intense is the ideal time to focus on this exercise.

Exercise 6: Slow down

Put a sticky note on your bathroom mirror that reads, "Today I commit to slowing down." When you make this commitment, you are deciding to honor the moment before you.

Here are some ideas that I personally use to help me slow down. Take a moment and see what else you can think of to help you in this process.

1. I slow down my pace when I notice that I am walking really fast.

2. I stop and sit down for a minute, close my eyes, and breathe when I begin to feel stressed.

3. I take time to skin brush or use a body scrub before a shower or bath.

4. I brush my teeth with consciousness, focusing on the movements of the brush against my teeth and gums and noticing how it physically feels.

5. I pick a dishwashing soap I love the smell of, being aware of the scent as I wash dishes. When I enjoy the smell of my environment, I notice I breathe more deeply.

6. I create ambience when I eat a meal by playing music, lighting a candle, placing pretty flowers on the table, or using "special occasion" dishes.

7. I sit in the car for five minutes before I go into a houseful of people after a full of day of work.

8. I take time to look the cashier in the eye at the store. Connecting to people for a moment or two really helps me slow down.

9. I listen to an audio book or relaxing music as I sit in traffic. As I focus on something that I enjoy in the moment, I notice my focus shift away from what I don't like.

Exercise 7: Create Love

Take a few minutes out of your day to take several slow, deep breaths. With your eyes open, look around and notice things surrounding you that you love.

Don't simply look at the things that catch your attention. Really focus on those things that give you a sense of calm or peace.

Take a breath, slow time down, and really *focus* on the things around you that you love. When you focus on things that you love, you begin to feel that emotion. Love is a very powerful feeling that feeds the connection to your Heart and helps it grow and thrive.

Affirmation:

I trust my Heart completely.

Notes

Notes

Notes

Notes

Notes

Notes

Notes

Notes

Notes

Notes

Notes

Notes

About the Author

Robin Lee is a medical intuitive and wellness coach residing in Southern California. For over two decades, Robin has been helping people all over the world build empowering relationships with themselves. She believes the body and mind are intimately connected and what we think and believe affect how we physically feel. Her clients' experiences show that if we listen to the body instead of trying to fix or control it, the healing process will go much faster.

Photo Credit: Rosemary Alexander

Printed in the United States
By Bookmasters